Job Hunting

C.V. Writing & Being Interviewed

By Linda Roshier
Second Edition
Black and White Version

First published by The Sales Career Academy, at Lynbyrd Express.
www.salescareeracademy.org courses@salescareeracademy.org

ISBN: 978-1-4467-4929-6

CONTENT

INTRODUCTION

I have been fortunate in my life to have met a variety of amazing people, many of whom did not realise how amazing and truly inspiring they actually are. I want to share just two stories of people who have inspired me to write this workbook in the hope that they might just inspire you.

Whilst training in a call centre I interviewed several people for an inbound telephone sales job. One young man was fortunate to be offered a job. He came along with a rucksack, a raw talent and a hunger to learn. After a few days of starting work he was found using the factory shower room, which many did especially those cycling to work, however he used it for cleaning his clothes as well as his body. It soon became apparent that he did this every morning. It turned out that this young man was homeless. Every day for a month he continued his routine until he got his first wage packet, then he went out and bought a new set of clothing. His skills in telephone sales developed and he became one of the Top Performers. Earning a good, steady wage he soon found himself somewhere permanent to live and continues to do well in the world today.

I had the privilege of taking part in mock interview skills with Year 11 students. One group of young ladies were refusing to be involved. Their stories ranged from school exclusions to being young carers, many had difficulties with reading and writing. We talked for a short while and they all went into the mock interviews. They overcame their fears by realising some of the skills and abilities they have. The feedback from those interviewing them was high praise indeed, the young ladies self esteem and pride in achievement was great – *"inflated as a hot air balloon!"* their teacher said.

When you are looking for work, the key is to neither over-exaggerate nor under value what you may offer an employer. Recognise the skills you do have and believe in yourself.
The pages within this workbook do not promise that you will find a job, however its aim is to give you the best opportunity to.

All the best, Linda Roshier

MODULE ONE - WHAT JOB?

As a people we tend to want to put other people and ourselves into 'boxes', and often make huge assumptions by the way someone looks, voice, race, gender and the like. We do not do this intentionally or with malice. The worse culprit of doing this to 'us' is usually our selves!

The main reason we limit our ambitions is because we do not recognise nor fully appreciate the knowledge, skills and abilities we actually have.

Once we do recognise and appreciate the knowledge, skills and abilities we have we can then start to consider what job we would

1. Like to do
2. Want to do
3. What most suits our skills and abilities

Quite often we have a Dream Job, this is usually the one out of reach and appears almost impossible to achieve, however it does not mean it is NOT achievable! It may be you have to start lower, gain qualifications and build a career in order to achieve the job you Dream of doing. Therefore bear this in mind, for example if you Dream of being a Vet you may still get a job working with animals whilst studying for Veterinary qualifications.

Firstly, go through the following examples of 'Transferrable Skills'. It is not an exhaustive listing however it will start to give you a good idea of what knowledge, skills and abilities you have and how they translate into the business world's terminology.

Once you have read through the Transferrable Skills examples carry out Exercise One.

TRANSFERRABLE SKILLS

BABY SITTING

Tasks and Duties	Transferrable Skills
Entertaining and Playing	Motivation, Creativity and Inspirational Skills
Preparing Drink and/or Food	Meeting Needs, Health & Safety
Getting ready for bed	Motivation, Selling, Communication, Supervisory, Organisation and Planning Skills
Putting to bed	Motivation, Selling, Communication, Supervisory, Leadership and Management Skills
Reading a story	Supportive Skills
Dealing with any arguments	Conflict Management, Influencing, Diplomacy Skills
Comforting	Approachable, Empathy and Leadership Skills
Following the parents instructions	Taking direction
Dealing with an situations as they happen	Decision making and problem solving skills

PARENTHOOD

Tasks and Duties	Transferrable Skills
Taking the kids to school on time	Time Management, Planning and Organising, Negotiating skills
Cleaning the home	Working on own initiative
Washing and Ironing	Presentation Skills
Household Income	Budget control
Using the computer	Computer skills
Dealing with illness	Care / Nursing and Counselling skills
Preparing meals	Decision making, budget, research and analysis, creative skills
Looking after the family	Coaching, Mentoring, Leadership and Management Skills
Organising a babysitter	Delegation skills.

TRAIN SPOTTER

Tasks and Duties	Transferrable Skills
Watching Trains	Monitoring, Planning and Organisation Skills
Logging details of trains	Administration Skills, possible computer skills in Word, Excel, etc.
Sharing information with others	Communication Skills, Computer skills if on internet.
Finding out where trains will be	Research, Investigation and Networking skills
Photographing trains	Creative skills
Picking the best place to sit and wait	Health & Safety, Patience, Analysis and Decision Making Skills.
Having a packed lunch	Pre-planning, Planning and Organisation Skills
Meeting with other train spotters	Networking Skills
Going through, checking and Updating information	Reviewing, Analysis, and Monitoring Skills

FOOTBALLER PLAYER

Tasks and Duties	Transferrable Skills
Cleaning Kit	Presentation and Preparation Skills
Making sure not offside side	Awareness and Attention to detail Skills
Passing the ball	Team working, Awareness, Influencing , Using Initiative Skills
Noticing how team are playing	Monitoring and Analysis Skills
Wearing shin pads	Health & Safety Skills
Taking note of coach / manager	Listening and Taking direction Skills
Getting past defenders	Negotiating Skills
Urging team on	Motivating and Inspirational Skills
Being captain	Supervisory and Leadership Skills
Communicating with the Referee	Negotiating Skills

HAIRDRESSER

Tasks and Duties	Transferrable Skills
Washing and Cutting Hair	Inter-personal and Customer Service Skills
Handling Complaints	Complaint Handling, Customer Service and Negotiation Skills
Making Appointments	Sales, Planning and Organisation Skills
Recruiting Staff	Inter-personal, Interviewing, Advertising and Decision Making Skills
Training Staff	Coaching, Mentoring and Teaching Skills
Keeping the Books	Accountancy, Record Keeping, Budgeting Skills
Ordering Stock	Telephone, Computer, Administration, Planning and Organisation Skills
Paying Staff	Payroll and Budgeting Skills
Taking Money	Money Handling, Organisation Skills

So what skills and abilities do you have?

The aim of 'Exercise One' is to recognise the skills and abilities that you have. It is worthwhile asking someone who knows you to help you complete this, as we can not always 'see' all of these in our self.

EXERCISE ONE: THIS IS ME!

In the following table write down as many 'Tasks and Duties' that you do as you can:

Tasks and Duties	Transferrable Skills

Once you have completed the list, consider the skills and abilities you need to do each Task and Duty. Consider what the 'business term' for that skill may be, then write those skills into 'Transferrable Skills'.

EXERCISE TWO: JOBS FOR ME!

The aim of this exercise is to give you a better understanding and recognition of the type of job that would best suit your skills, therefore give you a better opportunity to be considered by an employer.

Focus on the 'Transferrable Skills' you have listed in Exercise One.

Take a local newspaper or similar which lists all the different jobs being advertised. Then on the table below write down ALL the jobs in which your transferrable skills are mentioned.

Jobs	Like	Want	Best Suits Skills

Once you have completed the list of jobs, tick whether you 'Like', 'Want' that job and the jobs that 'Best Suit your Skills'. Those that you leave blank will be either the ones you do not like or do not want! Consider before you leave the exercise as to whether they actually suit your skills best and whether they may lead to a job you do want.

It is recommended that you repeat Exercise Two every job search session you do. This will enable you to focus on 'why' you are applying for a particular job role. Knowing why and how best that job fits your skills will enable you better opportunity to present your self.

It is worth taking some time to consider where job opportunities may be advertised.

There are all the standard places such as the Job Centres, Job Websites, Newspapers, Shop Windows, and Recruitment Agencies.

Have you ever considered other areas? For instance, who do you know? And do they know you are looking for work?

Social Networking is a great tool, have you heard the saying *"it's not what you know, but who you know!"*? We never quite know who knows who, or want they know, therefore it is always worth mentioning however ensure you keep the communication positive, upbeat, relevant and appropriate. Making sure that it does not become pestering or hassling.

Social Media, such as Facebook, Twitter or the business site LinkedIn, are also very good places.

A word of caution on Social Media sites such as Facebook: some employers have been known to view these sites, and page contents written by individuals have proven to be detrimental to their cause.

Furthermore, if there is somewhere you would really like to work there is no reason why you should not approach them directly whether they are currently advertising or not. Contacting them by letter or through their website with a copy of your C.V. (Curriculum Vitae) explaining why you would like to work for them is pro-active, it may not lead to a job interview however never say never! You do not know until you ask.

MODULE 2 – C.V. WRITING FORMS

When applying for jobs you do require Curriculum Vitae, a C.V., and there are many very good services and websites that give specialist help to put a C.V. together.

In addition there are many jobs which require you to also complete a Job Application Form; this may be in electronic format online or hand written.

Knowing what to write is the key to better opportunity.

C.V. WRITING

Your C.V. is your opportunity to shine. It is an opportunity for you to present yourself, your skills and abilities and give the employer a clear understanding of how you may meet the criteria for the job they are advertising.

Some people have a different C.V. for the different job types they apply for; highlighting the skills and abilities they have which match that specific job type. Others have a generic C.V. which they send to all jobs. Neither is right nor wrong, however it is most important that the content of your C.V. is honest and can be supported. For example, if you claim to hold a Degree in Biology have the qualification certificate to prove it.

A C.V. should include the following:
1. Your Name
2. Your Contact Details
3. Your Personal Information
4. Your Work Experience
5. Your Education
6. Your Interests and Activities
7. Additional Information

You may or may not choose to give a Personal Statement as well. Make sure your C.V. looks professional and is easy to read.

Sample of a C.V. Format

Your Contact Details:
Address
Telephone Number
Email

Your Name

Personal Statement:

Personal Information

Martial Status:
Nationality:
Place of Birth:
Location:
Date of Birth:

Work Experience

Education

Interests and Activities

Additional Information

Before you start writing a C.V. it is worth considering what an employer is looking for. This is the First Stage, and generally they are looking for whether or not a person matches their job criteria or specification: meaning, do they have the potential to be the 'right person' for the job.

At this First Stage it is important to be clear and concise about yourself, creating interest in you. The potential employer will not expect your C.V. to have all the answers that is what the interview is for. Generally potential employers / recruiters are looking for reasons to interview someone, rather than reasons not to interview someone.

The following is a guide to what you may write:

PERSONAL STATEMENT

This is an introduction to you, highlighting your key skills, abilities and experiences. Use your results from Exercise One here in a short summary. Keep it factual and professional, avoid using 'humour' and 'slang'.

For example:

I have very good communication and inter-personal skills, which enable me to offer good customer service whether on the telephone or face to face. I have experience in complaint handling and decision making.

YOUR NAME

This is your formal name, not your nickname or name you may go by generally. It is the name that will be on official documentation when you are employed.

YOUR CONTACT DETAILS

It is important that a potential employer and recruiter are able to contact you to invite you to interview, and to tell you the outcome of that interview. Therefore ensure the address and telephone numbers you give a current and correct.

YOUR PERSONAL INFORMATION

This is where you state your marital status, date of birth, nationality, place of birth and current living location.

What you state is personal to you: for example, some people choose not to give their date of birth because they feel that their age may be a barrier to being interviewed being deemed either too old or too young.

YOUR WORK EXPERIENCE

This is where you put your job history, starting with the last job first and working backwards.

The usual format for each job is:

> To and From Date – when you started and when you left
> Job Title
> Company Worked For
>
> Details of Job Role, Duties and Responsibilities

Some people also like to put in 'Successes' or 'Achievements'.

For example:

> November 2009 to October 2010
> **Cleaner**
> Lynbyrd Express, Hampshire
>
> Responsible for maintaining the cleanliness of the office, emptying of waste bins, cleaning desks and vacuuming. Ensuring the kitchenette area remained hygienic and all crockery and cutlery was washed up, dried and put away. Ensuring chemicals used were compliant to regulations and stored according to regulations.
> Maintaining a stock record and ordering of stock.
>
> Achievements:
> Employee of the Month Award September 2010.

Should you not have a job history, refer to your results from Exercise One.

It has been known for a mother returning to work to put as her Job Title 'Household Manager' and amongst her Roles and Responsibilities – Budget Control, Monitoring, Coaching and Supervising!

The employer is generally looking for 'career progression', which may mean going from being a 'Mid-field Football Player' to 'Team Captain' or a transfer to a more prestigious club.

The employer is also looking for the skills and abilities you have used before, and how you have used them. They are also wishing to get a 'flavour' of who you are: your personality, character and behaviours.

Gaps in job history do not usually deter potential employers / recruiters from interviewing you; however they usually require an explanation at interview. Some employers/recruiters, however, do require an explanation before interview.

Literacy skills are not necessarily a key here, the ability to pick key words in a business terminology is. Therefore it may be worthwhile asking someone to help you. Using a computer or typewriter will enable a better presentation than something handwritten.

YOUR EDUCATION

This is where you put the details of your education.

The usual format used is with an entry for each school, college or university attended:

> School / College / University attended
> To and From Date attended
> Qualifications with Grades achieved

This is also where you put details of other qualifications or awards achieved using the same format: albeit from distance learning, in-house training, work place qualifications, etc.

It may be the case that you do not have formal qualifications and you choose to leave this section out of your C.V. That is perfectly okay. A prospective employer may ask you about this at interview and some jobs may be dependant upon a minimal education level.

YOUR INTERESTS AND ACTIVITIES

This is where you put details of your hobbies and interests, along with achievements outside the work place.

For example:

> Knitting: Reading: Football: Painting:
> Gardening: Travelling: D.I.Y.: Athletics:
> Computers: Music: Woodwork: Decorating.

> Achievements: Best Painting 2009 at ....
>   Completed the Race For Life at .....

ADDITIONAL INFORMATION

This area gives you the opportunity to write other information about you which does not full under the other headings.

For example, you may wish it be known:

- that you have a clean driving licence
- that you are willing to travel
- that you are willing re-locate
- any monies you have raised for charity.

It is recommended that you put here positive, added value details about you.

EXERCISE THREE: CREATE YOUR C.V.

Using the guide to what you may write and the sample C.V. start to create your own C.V.

The sample C.V. has been set out over the next three pages to enable you to do a written draft. Best tip is that before you complete your C.V. is to ask another person to review it for you and with you.

Address:

Telephone Number:

Email:

Your Name

Personal Statement:

The Sales Career Academy at Lynbyrd Express

Personal Information

Martial Status:
Nationality:
Place of Birth:
Location:
Date of Birth:

Work Experience

The Sales Career Academy at Lynbyrd Express

Education

_____

_____

_____

_____

_____

Interests and Activities

_____

_____

_____

_____

Additional Information

_____

_____

_____

_____

MODULE THREE - JOB APPLICATION FORMS

These are specific to a company / organisation and are a standard requirement.

Job Application Forms may be required to be completed online or be handwritten.

Job Application Forms are a legal document which you do need to sign; therefore it is important you complete them honestly and with full disclosure.

Failure to do so may lead to a dismissal from a job you had been awarded based on the information you have supplied.

Likewise companies / organisations are under a legal obligation to give everyone an equal opportunity.

When completing a Job Application Form you will find it an advantage to have your C.V. at hand, in addition the results to Exercise One and Exercise Two plus the details of the job you are applying for.

The information required on a Job Application Form will be the same information you have on your C.V. plus there may be a requirement to answer some specific questions in more depth.

It is important to ensure you read all and any instructions on the Job Application Form, these may include:

- Completing the Job Application Form in Black Ink
- Using capital letters
- A request for an explanation of any job history gaps

Before writing on the actual Job Application Form it is advisable to do a draft version first, and before answering any question refer first to the Job Advertisement / Details and then to your C.V., Exercise One and Two results. Relate your skills and abilities to the actual Job Advertisement / Details wording: even using some of that wording if it is appropriate and relevant, and keeping your reply clear and concise.

For Example:

The Job Advertisement

Part-Time Sales Advisor / Shop Assistant.

We are currently looking to recruit a part time sales advisor to work in our Home appliance showroom, working Monday, Wednesday, Friday and Saturday from 9am - 3pm with some flexibility for school runs if required.

Duties of the role include:

Providing excellent customer service and maximising sales performance in store - identify and fulfil customer needs appropriately - ensure all presentation standards are up held within the store.

Preferred Skills & Attributes:

Previous experience in retail would be advantageous - must have excellent face to face communication skills - presentable with warm and welcoming manner - ability to work as part of a team - must be motivated and flexible.

Skills, Abilities and Experience from Babysitting

Tasks and Duties	Transferrable Skills
Entertaining and Playing	Motivation, Creativity and Inspirational Skills
Preparing Drink and/or Food	Meeting Needs, Health & Safety
Getting ready for bed	Motivation, Selling, Supervisory, Communication, Organisation and Planning Skills
Putting to bed	Motivation, Selling, Communication, Supervisory, Leadership and Management Skills
Reading a story	Supportive Skills
Dealing with any arguments	Conflict Management, Influencing, Diplomacy Skills
Comforting	Approachable, Empathy and Leadership Skills
Following the parents instructions	Taking direction
Dealing with an situations as they happen	Decision making and problem solving skills

Example of Job Application Wording

I have excellent face to face communication skills. I am approachable, empathetic and a team player. I have experience of Home Appliances and good influencing skills. I am organised, flexible, motivated and can motivate others.

Supporting Evidence

Details of Babysitting Job Role and Duties

Reference from the person you babysat for

It is important that you are confident in the description you are giving of yourself, that you are able to meet the details that you give.

Therefore ensure that when you evaluate your skills against the Job Advertisement you neither over evaluate nor under evaluate them. Best practice is to state facts.

Do not try to assume what a potential employer / recruiter is thinking or will decide about your application, base you thinking on what you know. Never *assume* because it makes an *'ass'* out of *'u'* and *'me'*!

It is vital that you are able to support the statements that you make. Therefore obtaining references wherever possible before you make an application will only enhance your confidence.

Never be afraid to ask someone for a reference, even if you have not actually worked for them someone you have a known for a while is able to give you a 'personal reference' – this would usually be a professional person such as a Vicar, Scout Leader, Teacher, Bank Manager, etc.

EXERCISE FOUR

The aim of this exercise is to give you opportunity to practice matching up Job Advertisements to Skills and Abilities.

1. Look at the Job Advertisement example
2. Look at the Skills, Abilities and Experience example
3. Consider the Transferrable Skills
4. Write a concise and clear Job Application Wording
5. Write down the Supporting Evidence Required.

The Job Advertisement

They are currently looking to recruit an Administration Assistant to join our busy office. You will be required to provide an efficient and effective support service to our Office Manager.

Main duties include:
Maintain efficient and accurate filing systems.
Accurately photocopy documents as required, to include copying of documents for clients.
Carry out ad hoc administration tasks as required.

Skills and experience needed:
At least two years previous office experience in an administrative role.
Numeracy and a good standard of education.
IT literacy - experience of using Word, Excel, Outlook.
The ability to work well under pressure.
The ability to work methodically and to deadlines, without compromising accuracy.
Team player with the willingness and enthusiasm to support the team.

Top Tip:

You may not have the previous experience requested in a specific job role; however you may just have the knowledge, skills and abilities. Therefore do not be deterred by the request for specific previous experience! Be bold and confident, apply and let the advertiser / recruiter make the decision.

Skills, Abilities and Experience from Parenthood

Tasks and Duties	Transferrable Skills
Taking the kids to school on time	Time Management, Planning and Organising, Negotiating skills
Cleaning the home	Working on own initiative
Washing and Ironing	Presentation Skills
Household Income	Budget control
Using the computer	Computer skills
Dealing with illness	Care / Nursing and Counselling skills
Preparing meals	Decision making, budget, research and analysis, creative skills
Looking after the family	Coaching, Mentoring, Leadership and Management Skills
Organising a babysitter	Delegation skills.

Additional space has been given as there are many other Task and Duties related to the role of Parenthood which are Transferrable Skills which you may wish to add.

The Sales Career Academy at Lynbyrd Express

Example of Job Application Wording

_____

_____

_____

_____

_____

_____

Supporting Evidence

_____

_____

_____

_____

_____

It is recommended that you repeat this exercise, with other job advertisements, until you feel confident in matching Skills and Abilities to Job Advertisements.

MODULE FOUR - LETTER WRITING

The final part of your initial presentation of you is the covering letter you send to a potential employer / recruiter. The skills and learning you have developed from writing your C.V. and Job Application wording can be applied in your letter writing, for the same principles apply.

As there may be many people applying for the same job it is important to give yourself the best opportunity to shine. The format in which you present your letter will say just as much about you as the content.

Your literacy and hand writing skills can be supported by the use of computer, word processor or typewriter. However it is important that the wording used is your own, the letter content is relevant to the Job Advertisement and the statements you make are supported.

LETTER WRITING ETIQUETTE

There are various ways in which a letter may be set out, however there are two etiquette rules on starting and ending a letter:

1. Dear *Mr Blogs* ... when you start with a person's name you should always end the letter with ... Yours sincerely

2. Dear *Sir or Madam* ... when you start without a person's name you should always end the letter with ... Yours faithfully.

A letter should contain:

1. Your contact details
2. Your name
3. The date
4. The name of the person you are writing to
5. The name and address of the company your are writing to
6. The subject your letter refers to
7. Your signature

The Sales Career Academy at Lynbyrd Express

Sample of a letter format

Your Contact Details:
Address:
Telephone Number:
Email:

Date:

Name of Person Writing To
Company Address

Dear …….. (Mr / Miss / Mrs …. Or Sir / Madam),

Re: …. Subject you are writing about / Usually Job Vacancy and
Reference Number.

Main content of letter

Yours (Sincerely or Faithfully)

Your name

Enc (if you are enclosing documents)

Top Tip:

*If you are sending documents ensure you keep the originals and send
photocopies.*

The Sales Career Academy at Lynbyrd Express

The following is an example letter using the example Job Advertisement on page 21 and the example Job Application Wording on page 22.

68 FreeAds Way
JobJob
Hampshire

9876543210
janedoe@mememe.com

19th January, 2011

Mr Joe Blogs
The Household Appliances Company
High Street
JobJob Land

Dear Mr Blogs,

Re: Part-Time Sales Advisor / Shop Assistant

Further to your vacancy advertised in the local newspaper on 19th January, 2011.

I have excellent face to face communication skills. I am approachable, empathetic and a team player. I have experience of Home Appliances and good influencing skills. I am organised, flexible, motivated and can motivate others.

Please find enclosed my C.V. and personal reference for your consideration.

I look forward to hearing from you in the near future with a view to an interview.

Yours sincerely,

Jane Doe

Enc. C.V. & Reference

EXERCISE FIVE

The aim of this exercise is to help you develop your letter writing skills.

Remember it is important to use your own wording and that you reflect the content of the Job Advertisement.

Using the sample letter format, construct a covering letter for the Job Advertisement in Exercise Four.

It is recommended that you review your letter with another person to gain their feedback and input on how you may improve the letter.

It is also recommended that you practice letter writing using a variety of different advertisements and the preceding exercises to gain confidence in your letter writing skills and abilities.

Top Tip:

If you are using a computer or word processor, and decide to use the 'spelling and grammar' check function ensure that the setting is on the correct language default.

For instance: at the bottom of the screen in 'Microsoft Word' it will state either 'English (United States)' or 'English (United Kingdom)'. By 'right clicking' on this you can change the default setting.

If you have already typed your letter you will need to highlight all your typed words before you change the setting. Most computers and laptops have an English (United States) default setting.

The Sales Career Academy at Lynbyrd Express

MODULE FIVE - PRE-INTERVIEW PLANNING AND PREPARATION

Before you attend the interview it is important to prepare for it, this will increase your ability to present yourself in the best possible way and will instil confidence, enabling you more opportunity to lessen any nerves.

Planning and preparation includes ensuring you know where the interview venue is and how you are going to get there in time.

PERSONAL PREPARATION

APPEARANCE

First impressions are very important; therefore ensure you are 'booted and suited' regardless of what job you are going for. It may be that an organisation has a relaxed dress code however that is only when you have been given the job! Being 'suited and booted' projects to the prospective employer that you are keen, have respect, have an understanding of professional behaviour, and you are taking the interview opportunity seriously.

Top Tips:

- ✓ *Clean body, hair, nails, teeth, clothes, shoes*
- ✓ *Smart clothing, suit, clean, ironed*
- ✓ *No facial piercings, minimum jewellery*
- ✓ *Tattoos are concealed*
- ✓ *Light make up, if any*
- ✓ *Subtle perfume / aftershave, if any*
- ✓ *Ensure mobile phone is turned off in the interview*

It is a fact that your appearance counts 78% of the first impression you make, therefore consider what impression of you would like to leave the prospective employer with.

ATTITUDE

Understand why you are attending the interview and why you want this particular job, even if it is not your first choice. Should it not be your first choice your attitude to the interview should be as if it is your first choice! On no account should your attitude, your approach be as second choice.

Recognise that this is a 'two way' interview:

1. The interviewer has recognised something in your application that matches their job specification; this is their opportunity to find out more about you;
2. You have recognised something in the interviewer's job advertisement that matches your job requirements; this is your opportunity to find out more about them and the job.

Be 'Assertive': which means being confident, knowledgeable, open minded, willing to listen and learn.

Do not be 'Aggressive': which means not being over confident, defensive, confrontational in challenging and questioning, close minded, not willing to listen nor learn.

Do not be 'Passive': which means not being under confident, too willing to please by agreeing with everything, unable to ask questions, too nervous to listen and understand.

Consider how your voice 'tone' sounds; practice not just what you say but 'how' you say it.

The Sales Career Academy at Lynbyrd Express

Top Tips:

- ✓ *Be confident that you have something the interviewer identified and likes*
- ✓ *You have earned the right to the interview; the right to be considered further for the job*
- ✓ *It is okay to ask questions, consider what is it you want to know from the interviewer*
- ✓ *Be open minded and willing to learn*
- ✓ *Be assertive*
- ✓ *Practice, practice, practice - voice tones; how do you sound?*

It is a fact that when you talk the impact and impression upon the person listening to you comes from:

    7% of the words spoken
    38% of the way in which the words are said
    55% of the voice tones sound.

Furthermore, the ratio just between the way in which words are said and the sound of the voice tone is:

    15% of the way in which words are said
    85% of the voice tones sound.

Therefore the way you sound is more important that the words that are spoken, the ways in which the words are spoken are more important than what you say.

ABILITY

Every job will have a 'Job Specification' which will tell you what job involves, the duties that will be expected of you should you secure the job; some jobs may also have a 'Job Competencies Matrix' this will tell you what the company / organisation considers as a 'Competent Performance'.

One of the areas that can affect attitude – confidence and behaviour – is how 'capable' you feel your ability to match the Job Specification and Competencies.   It may lead you to feel over or under confident, therefore you need to balance this whilst considering that many companies will be looking for someone who will 'develop' within the role, therefore they are not expecting someone to be a 'perfect' match!

Consider everything you have done and achieved so far in your life and then compare it to the Job Specification.

The following is an exercise will help you recognise two things:

1. Just how much experience you do have
2. How that experience matches the Job Specification.

You may find it useful to have someone help you with this as we all have 'blind spots', which are things other people see in us that we do not see or know. Therefore open your mind and approach in a positive frame of mind.

Top Tips:

- ✓ *It is important to listen to the input of others*
- ✓ *What others 'see' as your strengths, these may be the same as an interviewer may see*
- ✓ *Be aware of your opportunities for development, to learn more and improve*
- ✓ *An interviewer may also be interested in how you wish to development and improve*
- ✓ *Understanding how you may meet the job specification will instil confidence*
- ✓ *Giving examples to support your understanding may aid the interviewer to see how you meet the job specification.*
- ✓ *Focus on the positives.*

EXERCISE SIX: PART ONE – FOR STUDENTS

This exercise is a more in-depth look at Exercise One. The aim is to give more supportive substance, evidence to the skills and abilities you have by providing examples.

The person interviewing you will want you to verbally give supporting evidence of your skills and abilities by providing an example.

First, on the following sheet, write down everything you can think of that you have achieved and experienced.

The following are some questions to help you start:

- What activities or events have you been involved with outside of school?
- What sporting achievements have you had?
- What academic achievements have you had?
- Have you ever done any babysitting?
- What would the person you babysitting for say about you?
- What have you learnt whilst babysitting?
- What responsibilities or duties do you have at home?
- What have you learnt whilst carrying out these responsibilities or duties at home?
- Do you have a part-time job?
- What do you do in the part-time job?
- What responsibilities or duties do you have in the part-time job?
- What have you learnt whilst carrying out these responsibilities or duties at work?
- Have you had a 'work experience'?
- Have you gone to work with a parent?
- What have you learnt whilst on your work experience?
- What have you learnt whilst going to work with a parent?
- Are you a member of a club?
- What do you do at that club?
- What have you learnt whilst going to that club?
- What else have you done and achieved?

The Sales Career Academy at Lynbyrd Express

Experiences & Achievements	This shows that...?

REFRESHER

The world of business will have different words, terminologies or jargon for a lot of the experience, skills and abilities you will have displayed in your first part list.

For instance:

- o Baby Sitting – looking after some body, regardless of age, will require certain skills and abilities such as 'leadership and management skills', 'conflict management', 'inter-personal communication skills', 'approachability', 'rapport building', 'instilling trust', 'creativity', 'taking ownership and responsibility' to name but a few.

- o Working in a Shop – will involve skills and abilities such as 'customer service', 'money handling', 'inter-personal communication skills', 'conflict management', 'complaint handling', 'dealing with difficult people', 'leadership and management skills' to name but a few.

- o Being a Team or Club – will involve skills and abilities such as 'being a team player', 'leadership', 'communication', 'being a winner', 'dealing with difficult people', 'conflict management', 'dealing with defeat', 'understanding roles and responsibilities' to name but a few.

It is important that the preparation you do before the interview includes examples that relate to the Job Specification.

EXERCISE SIX: PART TWO – FOR STUDENTS

In the second part of this exercise acknowledge how capable you are, and consider how these are interpreted by employers.

Under the heading 'This shows that ...' write down what skills and abilities your experiences show.

For instance:

Experiences & Achievements	This shows that...?
Baby sitting for my neighbour	I am trusted I am able to take responsibility
Whilst babysitting the child started crying	I was able to comfort them I am able to deal with a difficult situation I managed a potential conflict situation.
Whilst working in the shop I dealt with a customer complaining	I was able to listen to the customer and solve her problem. I am able to do complaint handling.
I captained the Hockey Team to a win	I have leadership skills I understand 'team dynamics' – the different way people behave.

Top Tips:

- ✓ *Be confident in your capabilities*
- ✓ *Give examples to support 'which shows that...'*
- ✓ *Examples may include 'References' from people who have witnessed you displaying your skills and abilities.*
- ✓ *Ask someone you know to help you compile your lists; they will see things in you that you are currently unaware of.*
- ✓ *Prepare a personal 'Portfolio' wherein you put any and all certificates, qualifications and other achievements, references and anything else you believe is applicable to the job application including your c.v.*

It is important to recognise and acknowledge just how much skill and ability you do have; that you have a good foundation, a good base from where you will, if given the opportunity, develop into a valued employee.

EXERCISE SEVEN: PART ONE – FOR ADULTS

This exercise is a more in-depth look at Exercise One. The aim is to give more supportive substance, evidence to the skills and abilities you have by providing examples. The person interviewing you will want you to verbally give supporting evidence of your skills and abilities by providing an example.

First, on the following sheet, write down everything you can think of that you have achieved and experienced.

The following are some questions to help you start:

- What activities or events have you been involved with outside of the home?
- What sporting achievements have you had?
- What academic achievements have you had?
- Have you ever done any child minding?
- What would the person you child minded for say about you?
- What have you learnt whilst child minding?
- How have you managed the family finances?
- What have you learnt managing the family finances?
- Do you have a part-time job?
- What do you do in the part-time job?
- What responsibilities or duties do you have in the part-time job?
- What have you learnt whilst carrying out these responsibilities or duties at work?
- Have you had any family conflicts or difficulties?
- Have you had to motivate, support and encourage children / family members?
- What have you learnt whilst dealing with any conflicts or difficulties?
- What have you learnt whilst motivating, supporting and encouraging others?
- Are you a member of a club?
- What do you do at that club?
- What have you learnt whilst going to that club?
- What else have you done and achieved?

Experiences & Achievements	This shows that…?

REFRESHER

The world of business will have different words, terminologies or jargon for a lot of the experience, skills and abilities you will have displayed in your first part list.

For instance:

- o Child Minding – looking after some body, regardless of age, will require certain skills and abilities such as 'leadership and management skills', 'conflict management', 'inter-personal communication skills', 'approachability', 'rapport building', 'instilling trust', 'creativity', 'taking ownership and responsibility' to name but a few.

- o Family Finances – will involve skills and abilities such as 'budgeting', 'forecasting', 'money handling', 'inter-personal communication skills', 'leadership and management skills' to name but a few.

- o Conflicts & Difficulties – will involve skills and abilities such as 'inter-personal communication skills', 'counselling', 'understanding behaviours', 'dealing with difficult people', 'conflict management', 'dealing with defeat', 'understanding roles and responsibilities', 'management skills' to name but a few.

- o Motivating & Support – will involve skills and abilities such as 'inter-personal communications', 'strategic planning', 'goal setting', 'performance review', 'logistic planning', 'reward & recognition', 'management skills' to name but a few.

It is important that the preparation you do before the interview includes examples that relate to the Job Specification.

EXERCISE SEVEN: PART TWO – FOR ADULTS

In the second part of this exercise acknowledge how capable you are, and consider how these are interpreted by employers.

Under the heading 'This shows that ...' write down what skills and abilities your experiences show.

For instance:

Experiences & Achievements	This shows that...?
Child minding for my neighbour	I am trusted I am able to take responsibility.
Whilst child minding the child started crying	I was able to comfort them I was able to deal with a difficult situation I managed a potential conflict situation.
Managed the family budget	I was able to ensure we covered expenditures. I was able to identify a need in the family for an item, and then manage the budget so we could save for a particularly high cost item.
A neighbourhood dispute	I have leadership and management skills. I have influencing and negotiation skills I understand the different way people behave. I have conflict management skills.

The Sales Career Academy at Lynbyrd Express

Top Tips:

- ✓ *Be confident in your capabilities*
- ✓ *Give examples to support 'which shows that...'*
- ✓ *Examples may include 'References' from people who have witnessed you displaying your skills and abilities.*
- ✓ *Ask someone you know to help you compile your lists; they will see things in you that you are currently unaware of.*
- ✓ *Prepare a personal 'Portfolio' wherein you put any and all certificates, qualifications and other achievements, references and anything else you believe is applicable to the job application including your C.V.*

It is important to recognise and acknowledge just how much skill and ability you do have: that you have a good foundation, a good base from where you will, if given the opportunity, develop into a valued employee.

THE COMPANY / ORGANISATION

The Company or Organisation has given you an opportunity to interview for them; they have taken the time to find out about you by reading your application. Therefore they will be pleased if you have taken the time to find out about them.

With the use of internet it is advisable to use a search engine to find everything you can about the company or organisation you are interviewing for. Plus read everything they have sent through to you which may include Job Specification and Company Literature.

It is okay to take into the interview any notes you have made and to tell them what you have found out about them. Whilst carrying out this investigation is it likely that you have some questions you would like to ask them, therefore in your preparation write these questions down as it is okay to ask questions. Remember, this is a two way interview.

It is also recommended that you find out, where possible, what the companies 'Recruitment Process' is. For instance:

- How many people will be interviewing you;
- Who those people will be;
- What will the interview consist of.

There are some companies who carry out 'personality tests'; these are usually 'tick' box questionnaires, your answers are interpreted giving the interviewer information about you and your personality, behaviours, characteristics.

These are not something to be afraid of; there are usually no right or wrong answers. It is best to not think about the answer too much and complete the questions assertively. These are not something you can prepare for, other than having awareness; the results are usually quite interesting.

Knowledge underpins confidence.

QUESTIONING TECHNIQUES

The purpose of an interview is to find out as much information as is needed to make an 'informed' decision. As this is a two way interview, it is okay for both you and the interviewer to ask questions (usually you will be invited to ask questions after the interviewer has ask theirs).

Understanding the types of questioning techniques will enable you to make the most of your questioning.

OPEN QUESTIONS

These are questions that require an explanation as an answer.

Open questions start with How, What, When, Who, Where, What.

This type of questioning enables someone to talk and give information, which may lead to further questions being asked, this is called 'probing'.

CLOSED QUESTIONS

These are questions that require a Yes or No answer.

Closed questions start with Do, Are, Is, Would.

This type of questioning stops conversation therefore should be used to confirm or clarify something.

When asked a closed question just answer Yes or No, there is no requirement to give further information. If the person asking the question requires more information or an explanation they will ask a further open question.

When preparing questions for the interviewer consider:

- 'what is it you need to know'
- 'why you need to know it'
- the impression your question may give the interviewer

Remember throughout your voice tones.

For instance: you may want to know

- What are the training and development opportunities in the organisation?
- What the opportunities for job progression / career advancement?
- Do you get paid for overtime worked?
- What are the opportunities for overtime?
- Is weekend working expected?
- What are the company's social activities and events?

When you are in an interview all the questions you thought of before usually disappear from your memory, therefore it is recommended that you write your questions down and take them in with you.

Asking questions and having a prepared list of questions demonstrates further to the interviewer your organisation and planning skills, your interest in the job, as well as your ability to communicate effectively.

Top Tips:

- ✓ *Know why you are asking the question – what is it you need to know?*
- ✓ *Rather than go around the houses asking lots of questions, why not ask the question directly?*
- ✓ *Ensure your questions are neither rude nor intrusive.*
- ✓ *Quality questions are better than lots of questions.*
- ✓ *Beware of asking two or more questions at one time which may cause confusion and not get the information you need.*

EXERCISE EIGHT

The aim of this exercise is to provide you with a 'Library of Questions' and a 'Library of Answers' that you may use during mock interviews and actual interviews.

The danger of over practicing is that you can begin to sound 'scripted' and you lack the flexibility to respond to unexpected questions. Being too practiced may lead to you undermining your own ability to shine and your confidence, which is what we are trying hard to avoid!

It also enables you to build in consistency and competency during interviewing, as well as record and share with others good examples of Questions. Therefore this is an ongoing exercise.

To start building your Library of Questions: refer to the Job Advertisement on Page 21 and the Job Advertisement in Exercise Four, Page 23. Consider what is it you want to know, using the examples on Page 46 as a starter guide.

To enable you start building your Library of Answers there follows some questions that you may be asked in an interview and two examples of competencies matrixes.

- Tell me about yourself
- How would your best friend describe you?
- Tell me about a time when you worked as part of a team
- Tell me about a time when you were faced with an awkward situation, and what you did
- Tell me about a time when you came up with a good idea to solve a problem
- Tell me about a time when you delivered good customer service
- Why did you leave your last job?
- Please explain the gap in your job history.
- Where do you see yourself in 5 years time?
- What have you done so far towards this goal?
- When can you start work?

Interviewer questions often relate to a Competencies Matrix, this is a predetermined scale that shows what 'competent' looks like.

The Sales Career Academy at Lynbyrd Express

Below is an example of:
New Starter Inbound Telesales Operators Competencies Matrix

Activity	5 – Excellent	3 – Competent	1 – Poor
Planning for monthly target achievement	Always plans for monthly target achievement and executes. Always achieves target.	Plans for monthly target achievement, however does not always execute.	Target attainment is not planned for. Rarely considers the affect of holiday / training and so forth.
Self Discipline – maintaining focus	Always maintains focus and encourages others. Displays positive behaviour and attitude.	Maintains focus, not easily distracted.	Easily distracted. Displays negative behaviour and disruptive attitude.
Open Questioning Techniques	Always uses open, closed, probing and hypothetical questioning techniques appropriately and relevantly.	Uses Open Questioning however does not always probe.	Asks leading and / or multiple questions.
Matching Customer Needs	Summarises customers' need and links benefits back of an appointment to the individual.	Occasionally summarises customers' need and /or links benefits back of an appointment to the individual. Rarely does both.	Never summarises customers' need and / or links benefits back of an appointment to the individual.
Overcoming Objections	Is Assertive. Discovers true objection and overcomes it appropriately and relevantly.	Discovers at least one objection and overcomes it appropriately and relevantly.	Is Passive or Aggressive when objection is raised.
Gaining Customer Commitment	Consistently uses differently closing techniques to gain customer commitment. Always gives customer opportunity to appoint and/or arranges call-back.	Confirms customer's interest and mostly gives opportunity to appoint and / or arranges call back.	Rarely gives customer opportunity to appoint or arranges a call back.
Call Quality Assessment	Regularly achieves 100% on call assessments.	Achieves 80%.	Achieves 0 to 79%
Target Attainment	Consistent target beater / over achiever.	Consistent target achiever.	Struggles to hit consistently.

As a bit of fun, why not create your own Competencies Matrix for the job you do!

A Supervisors Competencies Matrix

Activity	5 – Excellent	3 – Competent	1 – Poor
Self Discipline	Consistently maintains focus and encourages others. Consistently displays positive behaviour and attitude.	Maintains focus, not easily distracted.	Easily distracted. Displays negative behaviour and disruptive attitude.
Personal Drive and Effectiveness	Consistent existence of a positive, 'can do' mentality. Consistently finds ways round obstacles in order to accomplish objectives.	The existence of a positive, 'can-do' mentality, anxious to find ways round obstacles in order to accomplish objectives	The existence of a negative, 'can not do' mentality. Rarely finds ways round obstacles in order to accomplish objectives.
People management and leadership	Consistent motivation of others towards the achievement of shared goals. Consistent establishment of professional credibility. Consistent creation of reciprocal trust.	The motivation of others towards the achievement of shared goals. The establishments of professional credibility and the creation of reciprocal trust.	Rarely motivates others towards the achievement of shared goals. Rarely establishes professional credibility. Rarely creates reciprocal trust.
Business Understanding	Consistent adoption of a corporate business perspective including accountabilities of business processes and operations, of 'customer' priorities and continuous improvement or transformational change.	Adoption of a corporate business perspective including accountabilities of business processes and operations, of 'customer' priorities and continuous improvement or transformational change.	Rarely adopts a corporate business perspective including accountabilities of business processes and operations, of 'customer' priorities and continuous improvement or transformational change.
Professional and ethical behaviour	Consistent possession of the professional skills and technical capabilities, knowledge and integrity that is required for effective achievement in the arena, simultaneously compliant with relevant legal and ethical obligations.	Possession of the professional skills and technical capabilities, knowledge and integrity that is required for effective achievement in the arena, simultaneously compliant with relevant legal and ethical obligations.	Rarely possesses professional skills and technical capabilities, knowledge and integrity that is required for effective achievement in the arena, simultaneously compliant with relevant legal and ethical obligations.
Communication, persuasion and interpersonal skills	Consistently has the ability to transmit information to others, both persuasively and cogently, displays listening, comprehension, empathetic and understanding skills.	The ability to transmit information to others, both persuasively and cogently, displays listening, comprehension, empathetic and understanding skills	Rarely has the ability to transmit information to others, both persuasively and cogently, displays listening, comprehension, empathetic and understanding skills.

LIBRARY OF QUESTIONS

LIBRARY OF ANSWERS

FINAL PREPARATIONS

It is usually wise to conduct a review of your preparations before you go to an interview and ensure you have everything you need.

The review should consist of:

- Reading through the Job Specification
- Ensuring you have the correct venue address and contact details
- Ensuring you have the correct date and time of interview
- Ensuring you have directions to the venue
- Ensuring you know the time you have to leave
- Preparing your clothing and cleaning your shoes
- Ensuring you have your prepared questions
- Ensuring you have ready any specific requirements made by the interviewer.

Depending upon the job role you are going for, you may also consider taking to the interview a Portfolio; along with a copy to leave with the interviewer.   The Portfolio may consist of:

- C.V.
- Certificates of Qualifications
- Awards and Achievements
- Letters of Referral or References
- Appropriate and Relevant Letters of Thank You, Recognition and Accomplishment

This is not always a requirement, however further demonstrates planning and organisational skills and may indicate to the interviewer the level of interest you have in the job role and in working for the company.

Taking an additional copy of your C.V. is recommended.

MODULE SIX - THE INTERVIEW

YOUR ARRIVAL

Ensure you arrive at the interview venue no later than approximately 10 to 15 minutes prior to the stated interview time. When walking into reception do so with head held high, positive strides and a smile on your face!

Arriving in good time will enable you to gather together your thoughts, attend to personal needs (for instance visit the toilets, get a drink of water, check personal appearance), and mentally prepare.

Beware that behaviours, particularly inappropriate behaviour or language, within the reception area prior to interview may be reported back to the interviewer(s). Many companies and organisations consider this as part of the interview process.

ENTERING THE INTERVIEW

When walking into the interview do so with your head held high, positive strides and a smile on your face!

Handshaking on meeting your interviewer(s) is acceptable business behaviour.

Eye contact demonstrates confidence and openness.

Your interviewer will usually introduce anyone else in the room, however should they not it is acceptable for you to ask providing you do so in a manner that is polite and professional.

You will usually be invited to sit down in a pre-determined seating arrangement. Ensure you sit up straight, no slouching! Shows interest.

DURING THE INTERVIEW

The interviewer, or their colleague, will be taking notes of your conversation whilst you are talking. This is a legal requirement and enables them to reflect upon you as an applicant when they are decision making.

The questions the interviewer asks will usually consist of two sets:

1. Pre-determined questions to the job competencies / specification – these are the same for every applicant

2. Particular to you questions – these are questions raised following review by the interviewer of your application form and /or C.V., and any other questionnaire you may have completed.

Further questions may be asked following the answers that you give.

You will also be given the opportunity to ask questions; it may be that the answers to your questions are given by the interviewer prior to this time, however further questions may arise from the information they give you.

Top Tips:

- ✓ *Bring questions with you, nerves and conversation will mean your mind will go blank!*
- ✓ *Bring your portfolio to the interview, including a copy of relevant information to leave with the interviewer.*
- ✓ *Before answering a question*
  Listen... Breathe... Think... Breathe... Answer.
- ✓ *If you do not understand a question, say so.*
- ✓ *If you do not know the answer to a question, say so – however consider a possible alternative / similar situation or experience you may answer with.*
- ✓ *Remember – manners maketh man; therefore 'please' and 'thank you' will always go down well.*

END OF INTERVIEW

When the interview comes to an end, it is okay to ask *'what happens next'*. The more progressive may even consider asking:

- Is there anything else you need to know to make a decision about me?
- How did I do in the interview?
- When may I start?

The interviewer will close the meeting; this is the time to give the interviewer a copy of your Portfolio if you have brought one with you.

Regardless of how you think the interview went leave the interview positively – with a smile, eye contact, hand shake and 'thank you', and positive strides. Carry the positivity on until you leave the building and turned the corner – can not be seen.

Making your own judgements and presumptions on how the interview went is okay, however rarely do we know what it is the interviewer is looking for. Therefore keep any disappointment and a 'jumping for joy' for the when you receive the decision/job offer.

It may be that following the interview you are uncertain as to whether this is actually the job / career for you. This is okay too; however consider what other information or experience of the job you require to make an informed decision.

MODULE SEVEN - AFTER THE INTERVIEW

When we leave an interview the first thing that happens is that we start trying to analysis what happened. Quite often we run into the danger of beating our self up on what we think we should have said, should have asked and should have done. Alternatively we may come away over-confident bolstered by a feeling that the interview went well for a job we really want.

This is the time to do a quick and honest self review. One of the best ways is to use the following framework. Do the exercise on an ordinary piece of paper.

What went well	What could have gone better	What I will do differently next time

The framework purposely only permits three answers and it is vitally important to recognise what you did well and as well as what could have gone better.

Once you have completed these two sections consider what you will do differently at your next interview. This then forms your personal Action Plan, and is the part you carry forward when you are planning your next interview.

Once you have completed this exercise screw up the piece of paper and throw it away. Its history! There is no point in beating yourself up over something you can neither change nor necessarily know to be true. Take forward the positive Action Plan into the next interview.

 www.salescareeracademy.org

A time frame is usually given on when you may find out the result of your interview this usually depends upon:

- The number of people being interviewed for the job
- The company's interviewing and decision making process.

Once this time frame has been reached, if you have not heard then it is okay to make contact with the company to find out the result.

Top Tips:

Should it be that you have not been successful on this occasion treat this disappointment positively:

- ✓ *Ask the company / interviewer for 'Feedback'*
- ✓ *Also ask for feedback on your interview performance and use your review feedback framework:*
  'What you did well', 'What you could have done better' – therefore you will have better understanding on your performance and how it was received, so you will know what to do differently next time and put it on your Action Plan.

The interview you have attended may be one of many, you may even be fortunate enough to be offered more than one job. Which one do you choose?

Usually you will know the job you like and want the most, however if you are having difficulty choosing refer back to your original selection process in Module One and Exercise Two. Consider the answers you received from your questions. Then make a choice.

Sometimes we are offered a job, however are still awaiting news from the job we really want. There is an old saying *'a bird in the hand is worth two in the bush'*. It may be you that you are waiting too long for something that may not happen; this is something only you can decide. However there is no reason why you can not phone the company and ask for a progress on the final decision making.

SUMMARY

An interview is an opportunity for you to shine. Different companies and organisations have different requirements; therefore the job advertisement and job specification are only the beginning.

There may be a number of other people interviewing for the same job, however they may not have the qualities and capabilities within the job specification that the interviewer is looking for.

Build your skills and abilities by carrying out 'mock' interviews.

Be confident in you; keep your 'self belief' positive.

Not everyone can be fortunate the first time. Did you know that Colonel Saunders (Mr Kentucky Fried Chicken) had to knock on a thousand doors before anyone would give him the time of day! Luckily for us he kept on going!

Happy Interviewing!

YOUR FURTHER DEVELOPMENT

To enable you to further develop your Job Hunting skills and abilities the following two pages contain a 'Learning Log' and an 'Action Plan'.

The Learning Log is so you may record your key points of learning, things you wish to remember.

The Action Plan is so you may record 'what you will do differently next time'. It will also enable you to see the improvement you are making. Occasionally it will show us that we are having a repeat of the same Action, when this happens revisit that module. Go through it again.

It is recommended that you go through this workbook at different intervals, as we become more experienced we can use that experience to gain further learning and 'tweak' our performance to become experts. Set your expectations realistically, at times it may feel as if you are eating an elephant however remember *the easiest way to eat an elephant is a bite at a time!*

To further develop your skills and abilities you may wish to read the Authors other publications.

Alternatively visit The Sales Career Academy's website www.salescareeracademy.org , enquire about courses at courses@salescareeracademy.org or visit the Sales Career Blog http://lynbyrdexpress.wordpress.com .

Authors other publications are:

The Art of Unlocking Your Potential
Published by Authorhouse Publications

The Sales Career Foundation Programme:
   Modules One & Two – Skills and Using Skills
Published via www.lulu.com

The Sales Career Academy at Lynbyrd Express

ACTION PLAN

ACTION	DATE COMPLETED	LEARNING

The Sales Career Academy at Lynbyrd Express

LEARNING LOG

DATE	LEARNING	HOW USING LEARNING

DO NOT QUIT

When things go wrong, as they sometimes will,
When the road you're tracking seems up hill,
When the funds are low and the debts are high,
And you want to smile, but have to sigh,
When care is pressing you down a bit,
Rest, if you must – BUT DON'T YOU QUIT

Life is queer with its twists and turns,
As every one of us sometimes learns,
And many failure turns about
When he might have won had he stuck it out!
Don't give up, though the pace seems slow
YOU MIGHT SUCCEED WITH ANOTHER BLOW!

Often the goal is nearer than
It seems to a faint and faltering man,
Often the struggle has given up
When he might have captured the Victors Cup!
And he learned too late when the night slipped down,
How close he was to the GOLDEN CROWN!

Success is failure turned inside out,
The silver tint of the clouds of doubt,
And you never can tell how close you are,
It may be near when it seems afar:
So stick to the fight when you're hardest bit,
IT'S WHEN THINGS SEEM WORST THAT YOU MUST NOT
QUIT!

Despite investigation the author of the Do Not Quit poem is unknown.

Printed in Great Britain by
Amazon.co.uk, Ltd.,
Marston Gate.